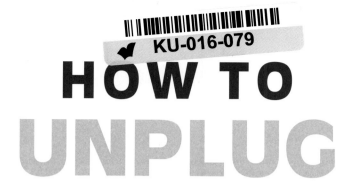

HOW TO UNPLUG

COMPUTER	**OFF** ⬤
IMAGINATION	⬤ **ON**

PHONE	**OFF** ⬤
ADVENTURE	⬤ **ON**

GET OFF YOUR GADGETS AND START ENJOYING REAL LIFE

ROSS DICKINSON

HOW TO UNPLUG

Vie Books is an imprint of Summersdale Publishers Ltd

Summersdale Publishers Ltd
46 West Street
Chichester
West Sussex
PO19 1RP
UK

www.summersdale.com

Printed and bound in Slovenia

ISBN: 978-1-84953-856-5

Substantial discounts on bulk quantities of Summersdale books are available to corporations, professional associations and other organisations. For details contact Nicky Douglas by telephone: +44 (0) 1243 756902, fax: +44 (0) 1243 786300 or email: nicky@summersdale.com.

HOW TO UNPLUG YOUR CHILD

101 WAYS TO HELP YOUR KIDS TURN OFF THEIR GADGETS AND ENJOY REAL LIFE

Liat Hughes Joshi

ISBN: 978 1 84953 719 3   Paperback   £5.99

DO YOU WISH YOUR KIDS WOULD UNGLUE THEIR EYES FROM THEIR SMARTPHONES AND COMPUTERS?

WOULD YOU LIKE A LITTLE BIT OF DOWNTIME FROM THE TECHNOLOGICAL TORRENT THAT EATS INTO OUR KIDS' EVERYDAY LIVES?

This sanity-saving collection of ideas and inspiration will help your children swap the screen for the sunshine and start getting more out of life. Split into bite-sized chapters, from fun indoors to activities on the go, food and cooking to science and nature, this book gives you and your kids a host of things to do after school, at the weekend and during those long holidays.

GET YOUR YOUR SH!T TOGETHER

HOW TO CHANGE **YOUR** LIFE BY TIDYING UP YOUR STUFF & SORTING OUT YOUR HEAD SPACE

VICKI VRINT

CONTENTS

INTRODUCTION

WHY UNPLUG?

SCREEN OFF ◯

LIFE ◯ ON

We're pretty lucky, when you think about it. Just twenty years ago, the personal computer was a luxury. Today, it's as commonplace as a toaster or a kettle, and as utilised as a car or a television. And that's not all. Smartphones, tablets, wireless connections, mobile data, MP3 players, clouds, online gaming, video-calls, streaming and office-style software are all there for us, right at our fingertips, should we ever need or want them.

The digital revolution has been, and continues to be, something quite beautiful. Never has knowledge been so accessible to so many at such little cost. Never has such a vast array of information been so easy and so rapid to attain. Never has communication been so effective and so simple. The digital revolution hasn't just been a game-changer or even a life-changer. It's a world-changer. And we're living right in the thrilling midst of it.

Perhaps it's because it's all so new, so exciting and just so remarkably *attractive* that, at times, it can feel to many of us that we are drawn to the online world a little more often than we should be. Have you ever walked down the street and found yourself stepping aside while another pedestrian strides forward, oblivious to everything but the smartphone in their hands? Have you ever picked up an e-book reader and found yourself suddenly missing the weight and smell of a well-thumbed paperback? Have you ever been in conversation with someone, only to have that conversation disrupted by the

inimitable beeps of an incoming text message?

If you have, and if you've also ever felt a little suspicious that we're all beginning to spend just a bit too much time online, then you won't be surprised by the recent studies and surveys which reveal that our general customs and habits are pointing that way.

One report from the communications regulator Ofcom shows that adults in Britain currently spend on average more time using their technological devices each day (8 hours and 41 minutes) than they do sleeping each night (8 hours and 21 minutes). Another study has revealed that, with the rise of smartphones and tablets, we spend twice as much time online as we did just 10 years ago, and that, of this time, 28 per cent will be devoted to social networking. With roughly 20 hours online each week, about 2.5 hours of that will be spent 'online while on the move' (utilising the internet in various capacities while away from home or work), which perhaps explains why you're having to avoid all those pedestrians with eyes fixed on their phones.

If you're holding this book in your hands (or reading it on the screen of an e-book reader), then it's likely that you're looking for ways to unplug. And, if you are, then this is exactly the book for you. Packed with a collection of ideas, activities and suggestions, it's guaranteed to motivate you to switch off your gadgets and get more out of life – to unwind, recharge and reconnect with the people, and the world, around you.

NO-PHONE-TIME CHALLENGES

Does your phone spend more time in your hand than in your pocket? Does it ping at you relentlessly? Do you find yourself checking it even when it doesn't ping, just in case it's been accidentally switched to flight mode? Then you might need a little extra help to unplug. Throughout this book, look out for the No-Phone-Time Challenges scattered among the suggested ideas and activities for unplugging. These will motivate even the most committed smartphone addicts to free themselves from the lure of the touchscreen.

CHAPTER 1

EXPLORE YOUR WORLD

COMPUTER OFF |||

IMAGINATION ||| ON

INTRODUCTION

Travel is a glorious thing, but not everyone can afford long plane trips or extended holidays from work. Yet you don't need to journey halfway across the world to travel. In fact, travel begins the moment you step outside your own front door. Whether you remain within the borders of your county or even within the borders of your town or village, you will likely be surprised by just how much is out there to discover for the first time. And – once you do discover it – you'll almost certainly want to discover more…

TURN RIGHT

DIFFICULTY: ▪◻◻◻◻

This is a fun game, and all it needs is some form of transport – perhaps your car, your bicycle, or even your feet. The rules are simple:

> 1. Start your car, get on your bike or begin walking.
> 2. Each time you reach a junction, you can only keep going forward or turn right.

It's deceptively simple, but – and here's the thing – you will eventually end up somewhere you've never been before. Once you're there, get out and have a look around. Explore. You may find there's a hidden gem of a place *right* around the corner.

'Turn Right' can be a fun game to play with your family or with a group of friends, as you take it in turns to decide at each junction. The results can be astonishing. I once played it in a car with my family, and ended up at a seal sanctuary. I've also played it on foot with friends during a night out after we grew bored of the pub we were in – 'Turn Right' eventually led us to what is now one of my favourite bars, but one which I never would have discovered otherwise.

VISIT THE LOCAL PARK

DIFFICULTY: ▪◻◻◻◻

Parks, greens, heaths, commons, playing fields,
recreation grounds… Whatever you call them,
the possibilities for exploring beyond our own
front doors are endless. Find the five closest
to you and visit them. You might want
to take a picnic, your dog, a kite or a
bag of nuts to feed the squirrels,
or you might just want to take
your own thoughts.

RECONNECT WITH THE PAST

DIFFICULTY: ▪▪◻◻◻

An underrated marvel of the modern world is our ability to preserve our history and heritage. In fact, local sites of historic interest are so prevalent in this country that it's likely you walk or drive past one every single day without even realising it's there. Start by visiting those that are easy to find – your local museum or town hall, perhaps. Then range further afield – country houses and old churches are magnificent repositories of history. Once you get a taste for it, search out those hidden gems in your vicinity: the Neolithic tombs, the medieval mosaics, the *fin-de-siècle* paintings, or the blue plaques denoting who once lived and breathed and worked in that very building. Such a pursuit can be a rewarding and educational glimpse into the past.

FORAGE

DIFFICULTY: ▪▪▮▯▯

Reconnect with your primal hunter-gatherer instincts by indulging in a spot of foraging. Whether it's by picking the berries, fruits and edible plants which grow wild along your nearest country lane, collecting mussels or small fish or crabs from a rock pool, or even hunting rabbits, squirrels or pigeons, foraging can be a sublime way of engaging with the ecological world around you. Not only will you provide yourself with a free and carbon-neutral meal or two, you'll develop an intimate understanding of your local environment and its flora and fauna as they change throughout each season. If you're unsure where to start, foraging guidebooks offer a wealth of information, or if you prefer to learn through example there are many self-employed foraging guides whose job it is to impart their knowledge to anyone interested. Guides are particularly helpful when you are learning what *not* to eat – you should maintain a healthy caution when foraging and eat only what you are sure is safe.

GO CAMPING

DIFFICULTY: ▪▪◻◻◻

For many people, 'going camping' brings to mind long drives to faraway campsites, three or four hours spent battling the elaborate complexities of pitching a tent, and wet, sleepless nights where the noise of nearby campers is only masked by endless and soaking rain. Yet, these days, camping can really be as simple or as extravagant as you want it to be.

At the cheaper end, SOUTSing (Sleeping Out Under The Stars) is fast gaining popularity among groups of friends who like to take some sleeping bags out to a nearby field or even a back garden and then enjoy together the night-light-show of the constellations above. For those who prefer shelter but still want to do it on the cheap, a simple pop-up tent can be bought from most supermarkets for no more than twenty pounds, and can be erected in a matter of seconds.

On the other side of the guy rope, there are plenty of ways to camp like a Mughal emperor. 'Glamping' – glamorous camping – found its way into the dictionary precisely because it is such a prevalent pursuit. If you'd rather swap your sleeping bag and roll of lino for an air-conditioned yurt with king-size beds, carpeted floors and a full-time chef who will cook you three-course meals on demand, there are plenty of companies out there who can grant even your choicest desires.

EXPLORE YOUR NATIONAL HERITAGE

DIFFICULTY: ▪▪▫▫▫

In my home country, the UK, there are numerous institutions which preserve the nation's heritage and landscapes, such as the National Trust or English Heritage. And, while everybody knows about them, very few take advantage of them. This is not an exclusively British phenomenon. Australia likewise has its own National Trust, in the USA there is the Royal Oak Foundation, and there are many more such organisations in countries all around the world. If you want to spend more time exploring your country, you can do no worse than utilising these institutions as your starting points. There are often plenty of sites you can visit for free, but a membership fee is sometimes necessary to join – though it's much less than you might think, and with it you will have full access to a stunning array of houses and buildings, gardens and parks, sites and monuments, as well as vast swathes of countryside and coastline.

BEACHCOMB

DIFFICULTY: ▪▪◻◻◻

Combing can be done on any beach – whether it's a fine stretch of coastline or the few centimetres of silt you can find on the banks of a river – and you'll be delighted and astonished at what you can find deposited there by the water.

Things to look out for:

○ **Old artefacts** – such as bottles, jewellery or coins which may give clues about the history of the area.

○ **Driftwood** – if you can carry it home, this can create a beautiful decoration, either as it is or made into something unique and spectacular such as a novel picture frame.

○ **Rock pools** – look closely, and you'll realise that these are ecosystems-in-miniature with their own individual arrays of life at various stages. You can take a pocket-sized book with you to help you discover which creatures you're looking at.

○ **Fossils** – if you can get to the south coast of England, especially in and around Dorset, there are still thousands of fossils waiting to be discovered. Again, a handy guidebook will help you identify what the fossils are, and which are the best fossil-bearing rocks.

○ **The supremely unusual** – the wonderful thing about beachcombing is that you'll never know just what you'll find. One man who regularly combs Porthcothan beach in Cornwall once found a series of pieces from Russian and Chinese spacecraft!

CHAPTER 2

EXERCISE YOUR BODY

SLOBBING	OFF
ENDORPHINS	ON

INTRODUCTION

Though exercise is fundamental and, for many people, an everyday part of life, in our increasingly sedentary world it can often seem that both the time and the inclination to exercise are non-existent. There are so many reasons not to exercise. Gyms can be intimidating places for the uninitiated. A jog from your house might fill your lungs with the smog of car exhaust fumes. After a full day of work, you simply might just not have the energy. But there are plenty of ways you can exercise and stay healthy without being a gym-rat or having the latest fitness apps. In fact, try out any of these suggestions and you won't just feel healthier – you'll have fun, too.

WALK

DIFFICULTY: ■■◻◻◻

Every country in the world offers huge possibilities for walking. In the UK, for example – even if it's central London – you'll be sure to find a public footpath or bridleway worth ambling along somewhere near your home. Research is never a bad thing, and you might want to peruse a website or two before setting off to discover the best walks in your radius. But once you've done your research, ditch your Fitbit, pedometer or smartphone app and just walk.

Whether you're after a 20-minute stroll along a riverside towpath or a three-day hike through the foothills of a mountain range, a good walk is rarely more than half an hours' drive away. If you try a few local walks and get a taste for it, there are plenty of longer tracks which are specifically designed for walkers – in the UK, we have the 630-mile South-West Coastal Path which begins at Somerset's Minehead and ends at Dorset's Poole; or the 270-mile Pennine Way which stretches from the picturesque Edale in the Peak District right up to Scotland. Don't be mistaken – these are both arduous and time-consuming treks, and if you're unable to devote all of your holiday time to them, then they can be undertaken (and undertaken rather pleasantly) in stages. A host of part-time walkers spend one weekend a year – sometimes with friends, sometimes with just their own thoughts – marching successive stages of a long trek. And, for many, it's the best weekend of their year.

RUN

DIFFICULTY: ▪▪□□□

If walking is too slow for you and you're itching to travel at greater speeds, running is a healthy, effective and carbon-neutral way of exploring your environment. If you haven't had a decent run since your schooldays, it's best to ease back into it – the NHS-sponsored Couch to 5k challenge is the perfect running plan for beginners. And then, once you've found your legs, running can be both strengthening and meditative. If you can manage it, try a run first thing on a Sunday morning as the sun is rising. It'll feel like the world belongs to you.

CYCLE FOR PLEASURE

DIFFICULTY: ▪◦◦◦◦

Can you remember your first ever bike? Was it a BMX, a shopper, or maybe a mountain bike? Did you adorn it with frills such as reflectors, new pedals or spokie-dokies? Was it your prize-possession, lovingly cleaned of the week's grime and mud every Sunday? Did you carry a puncture-repair kit and bottle of 3-in-1 oil in case of breakdown emergencies on long bike rides with your friends? There's a reason we used to love our bicycles so much. Before we could drive, they were our ticket to true liberation. They were our *wheels*. Try dusting off and oiling up that old bike sat in your garage; or, if you don't have one, buy a cheap, second-hand bike and refit it to your own specifications. Then go for a ride. Whether you fancy replacing your normal drive to work with an eco-friendly alternative or want to explore your local environment with friends or a partner, or even just find a different and leisurely way of getting out and about, getting back into cycling is the perfect way of reclaiming one of the joys of youth.

CYCLE FOR FITNESS

DIFFICULTY: ▪▪▫▫▫

Any form of cycling is generally a great cardiovascular workout, no matter how leisurely. However, if you really want to step it up a gear (no pun intended), cycling can be as active and as strenuous as you like. Many sports centres have velodromes for those who like to cycle competitively and want to improve their form and speed. Or, if you want to get off-road, mountain biking is rewardingly exhilarating, and can be undertaken anywhere from your local woods to distant mountain ranges. Could you even be a long-distance racer? Then grab your trusty steed and start practising road biking – who knows, you could compete in the next Tour de France!

TRY SILLY CYCLING

DIFFICULTY: ▪▪◻◻◻

Here's one final form of cycling for those who don't like to take things too seriously – silly cycling. Unicycles and penny-farthings are just two of the weird kinds of cycles readily available for those who fancy a challenge, albeit a slightly silly one. And, if you get good at it, you might want to get involved in the emerging scene of clubs, societies and even races for those dedicated to their weird and wonderful machines.

NO-PHONE-TIME CHALLENGE

When you're at a restaurant or in the pub with friends, agree that you will all pile your phones in the centre of the table. The first person who reaches for their phone has to pay for all the drinks.

LEARN A MARTIAL ART

DIFFICULTY: ▪▪❚❚❚

Learning a martial art isn't just an effective means to get fit and stay healthy, it's also a great way of building confidence through self-defence. While karate and judo are still the most popular and easily accessible martial arts studied across the country, if you look a little deeper you'll find a whole host of different methodologies – from ju-jitsu to capoeira, tae kwon do to aikido, kendo to muay thai – which utilise varying strategies and muscle groups. If you're keen to begin but don't know where, perhaps enrol for a taster session in a few different disciplines and then, through experiencing each, you'll be able to discover which is the right one for you.

JOIN A LOCAL SPORTS TEAM

DIFFICULTY: ◼◻◻◻◻

When people think of local sports teams, they tend to think of just one sport. The national sport. Football. And, for those of us who were never any good at it in school, the prospect of joining a football team can fill us with dread. But, of course, there are so many different sports and games out there and – as a result – there are so many different teams and clubs which are always on the lookout for new members. Have a look at this selection on the opposite page and see if any of them appeal to you:

rugby
hockey
tennis
cricket
darts
pool
ice hockey
basketball
archery
fencing
snooker
water polo
table tennis
squash
volleyball
trampolining
netball
rowing
sailing

SURF

DIFFICULTY: ▪▪▮▯▯

Have you ever wanted to surf, but just don't know how? You can try it, and you might be amazing, but don't be disheartened if you're not. Surfing is difficult and can take years to perfect, but it's not the only option when it comes to riding the waves. Why not try body-surfing? All you need is a shore break and your own arm power. Simply stand in the surf and wait for a wave to come. When it does, launch yourself into it and swim with all your might. You'll be surprised at how quickly the wave takes you and pushes you forward, so that you're surfing without the need for a board.

Here are some other alternatives to surfing:

BODYBOARDING

This involves a foam board approximately half your length which you can surf waves on while lying down. A good pair of flippers attached to your feet can push you out back beyond the break so that you can catch the really meaty waves.

PADDLEBOARDING (OR 'SUPPING')

If there are no waves at your nearest beach, you can easily rent a longboard upon which you can stand up (or 'sup') and use a paddle to push you out into the sea. You can still ride waves while supping by paddling into and then on them, but this is best when the waves are only a foot high or less.

RELIVE OLD CHILDHOOD GAMES

DIFFICULTY: ▪◻◻◻◻

There's a reason why, when we were kids, we used to spend so much time outdoors playing games. It's because they were so much fun. Whether you were the king of hopscotch or the queen of hula-hooping, or you spent hours with a skipping rope or Frisbee, or your games of tag or Marco Polo lasted an entire afternoon, there will doubtless be plenty of your old childhood games that are waiting to be rediscovered. Why not try one or two of them again in your garden or the local park, with friends or even alone? Not only will you delight in their simple pleasures, you'll also burn off a ton of calories at the same time.

NO-PHONE-TIME CHALLENGE

There are plenty of apps available which can block your web browser or social media sites so that you cannot use them on your phone for a set amount of time. The apps vary depending on your operating system and what aspects of your phone you would like to lock, but 'Freedom' and 'Anti-Social' are both good examples.

CHAPTER 3

EMBARK ON NEW ADVENTURES

TABLET	OFF ⬤
ADVENTURE	⬤ ON

INTRODUCTION

Films are becoming more and more visually spectacular; the internet is filled with the creative and the bizarre; computer games are hugely immersive and increasingly realistic; television programmes have become so addictive that we now have the term 'binge-watching' to describe the consumption of an entire box set in a short space of time (something which, let's be honest, we've all done at least once). With such a vast array of new and novel experiences available on demand, ready and waiting for us to plug into, it can be very easy to immerse ourselves in the digital world. But if you leave your house you'll find that, out in the physical world, there are more fun and unusual things to do with your free time than ever before. Why not take a risk and try something you wouldn't normally do? Something wacky or different. You never know, you might be on the brink of discovering your new favourite pastime!

TAKE ON THE ZOMBIES

DIFFICULTY: ▪▪◻◻◻

You're muscled into a dimly lit room. To your left stand three children and a wide-eyed woman. To your right, three young and joking men. The single bulb above you bursts with an electric flash, and its light is replaced by a flashing red beam as a siren wails its way into your eardrums. A mechanical whirr kicks in, and with a harsh clunk the trapdoor before you begins to open, sending thwacking shudders throughout the room. A barely perceptible hand claws its way out beneath the door, dragging through a limp body, followed by others. Zombies. They pull themselves to their feet, and approach. With a crash, a second door opens and twelve Kevlar-clad soldiers spill in, positioning themselves between you and the zombies, their guns aimed high.

'Move! *MOVE!*' they shout, and you follow them off through an industrial labyrinth of metal rooms and barren landscapes, always aware of the zombies, who follow with dogged footsteps, and who pick off the soldiers one by one, until it is left to you, you alone, to stand up and fight…

Live-action zombie experiences straddle the line between theatre and gaming, and are becoming ever more popular. The 21st-century version of a murder-mystery party, they are carefully crafted to give participants a sense of what it might be like to live through a zombie apocalypse, with actors playing the parts of both zombies and soldiers to lead you through an engaging and exceptionally fun narrative arc in which you are the main character.

Be warned: they are thoroughly immersive and therefore not for the faint of heart. But they can also be the most fun you've had in a long time.

WING-WALK

DIFFICULTY: ▪▪▮▮▯

If you really want to break away from staring at a screen, one excellent way to do this is by clambering onto the top wing of a vintage biplane, being strapped on to a pole sticking out the top of it, and watching in amazement as the ground drops away beneath your feet and the whole countryside lies below you like a model railway set. Although it's not an experience that comes cheaply (think in the region of £400 for the average wing-walking experience), the thrill is one you're unlikely to forget in a hurry.

GO WINE-TASTING

DIFFICULTY: ▪▪▫▫▫

All right, so Britain might not be the country which most people associate with good wine, but you'd be surprised at how many vineyards there are here, and how many are producing wines which are beginning to win awards and garner international attention. Here's a list of just a few in the UK which are definitely worth a visit:

- ▶ Biddenden Vineyards, Kent
- ▶ Purbeck Vineyard, Dorset
- ▶ Three Choirs, Gloucestershire
- ▶ Camel Valley, Cornwall
- ▶ Glyndwr Vineyard, Glamorgan, Wales
- ▶ Ryedale Vineyards, Yorkshire
- ▶ Adgestone, Isle of Wight

Most vineyards offer various activities to make your visit as immersive and interesting as possible – from touring the vines and learning about the different types of grape and the process of winemaking itself, to tasting a wide variety of wines and being tutored on how to spot the nuances between each. And, of course, there will be plenty of wine to buy at the end (often at a reduced rate if you've paid an entry fee), so you can continue the tasting at home!

GO COASTEERING

DIFFICULTY: ▪▫▪□□

If you love swimming in the sea, rock climbing or cliff jumping, coasteering provides an energetic and enlivening amalgamation of all three. Coasteering teams regularly take to their local coastlines, where they dress themselves in wetsuits, gloves, boots and helmets, and then work together to explore those points where the sea meets the land. There are many different opportunities for coasteers from the first-timer to the headily experienced. If you're new to it and have a healthy respect for the perils of wild water, start where the shorelines are long, calm and fringed by little more than lapping ripples. Or, if you fancy something a little more dramatic, find an ocean coastline. There you'll find the cliffs and the plunge pools, the gullies and the impact zones, the waves and the beaches inaccessible by road, all waiting for you to discover, raw and elemental, in a thrilling combination of sea, sand and stone.

GO PAINTBALLING

DIFFICULTY: ▪▪◻◻◻

Gather your friends and select a Saturday or Sunday which you all have free. Find your nearest paintball location and book yourselves in. Whether you take it with po-faced seriousness or just as a bit of fun, an afternoon paintballing with your comrades beside you, fighting together for survival, can be both entertaining and enlivening. If you have a low pain threshold and don't fancy the prospect of being on the receiving end of whizzing pellets of paint, Laser Quest is an entirely pain-free alternative, and can be just as fun. Some Laser Quest zones even have outdoor areas, so you can recreate the strategic thrill of a game of paintball with guns which fire only harmless rays of light.

GO TUBING

DIFFICULTY: ▪▪◻◻◻

Invest in an inflatable inner tube (the bigger the better – try the inner tube of a tractor tyre, if you can). Get some friends to do the same. Find a river. Take two cars. Park one at the start and the second at the finish. Launch yourself into the river at the start, atop your tube. Float down to the finish. If the river flows slow, take food in a sealable bag and keep it in your lap, and take beers in another bag which you can suspend off the tube and into the river to keep them cool. Eat and drink at your leisure. If the river flows fast, dispense with the food and drink and make sure you can hold on. Either way, enjoy a view of the countryside which you'd never see otherwise. At the end, dry yourself off, climb into the car you've left at the finish, and then do it all again.

GET WILD WITH THEATRE

DIFFICULTY: ▪◦◦◦◦

Wild theatre is positively booming throughout Britain's more rural areas. Unlike traditional theatre companies, which tend to hold their performances in buildings, wild theatre companies take their audiences on an outdoor adventure, creating a thoroughly immersive experience which is not just about the show itself, but is a means of transporting you to another world. If you find traditional theatre intimidating or alienating, wild theatre can be a wonderful new way of accessing drama – and who knows, you might even find yourself so drawn into these outdoor shows that you want to start going to the traditional theatre, too! And, if you want to take the interaction one step further, why not join a wild theatre company? It doesn't matter how well you can act – amateur theatre companies are always on the lookout for people willing to play minor roles or help out behind the scenes with set design, costumes, make-up or music.

GO ZORBING

DIFFICULTY: ∎∎∎◻◻

Do you remember, as a child, the simple joy of rolling down a hill? Zorbing takes it to the next level. Ensconced in the protective wrapping of a large inflatable ball (the 'zorb'), you can recreate that childhood delight of hill-rolling without fear of breaking a bone or two (because, whether or not you like to admit it, you're just not as *bendy* as you were when you were seven). Zorbing has become an increasingly popular pursuit, and you can find opportunities to zorb all over the UK. For an extra thrill, you can even zorb on lakes (perfect for anybody who fancies walking on water), though I would strongly recommend that you don't do it in the sea – a rip current or strong wind could find you paddling your way back from the Arctic.

NO-PHONE-TIME CHALLENGE

Give your phone to a friend and make them promise not to give it back for a set amount of time, no matter how much you beg.

CHAPTER 4

EMBRACE YOUR SOCIAL LIFE

TELEVISION	
GOOD TIMES	

INTRODUCTION

Remember at school when you couldn't wait to see your friends every morning? When all you wanted to do was just hang around and be with your mates? When you didn't need beer or coffee or lunch dates or anything but each other's company to spark a long and in-depth conversation? Good friendships never die, they just get ignored. One of the most common regrets people claim towards the end of their lives is that they didn't spend more time with their friends and family. But it's so easy to rejuvenate those friendships with a minimum amount of effort. Or, if you're on the lookout for new friends, it's never been easier…

ARRANGE TO SEE AN OLD FRIEND

DIFFICULTY: ▪◦◌◌◌

This requires no explanation and is ludicrously simple to achieve. But it's included in this book because, as lives progress and paths diverge, it can be very easy to go weeks, months or even years without seeing that one person who, back when you were teenagers or young adults, you couldn't live without. So, even if it does require a conscious effort, decide to make time for them, regardless of whether that time is half an hour at a coffee shop or a weekend in Amsterdam. And if you're worried that they feel you've been neglecting them lately, stop it. In all honesty, they're probably worried that you feel *they've* been neglecting *you*.

PLAY DINNER CAROUSEL

DIFFICULTY: ▪▪◻◻◻

To play Dinner Carousel, you will need four friends and one week. Throughout that week, each of you will host a dinner party. Simply designate the friends you'd like to play with, and then pick one night each during the week when you will visit each other's houses, and when the host will, well, host. You can anonymously rate each other if you like and even award a prize to the winner at the end of it all, or you can just treat it as a good excuse to regularly get together with your friends and enjoy what culinary delights they have to offer. And, if a full week of flamboyant meals every night sounds too much for you, Dinner Carousel can also be played over a month, with your visits to each other's houses taking place every Thursday night, for example, until you've all had a chance to be the host.

JOIN A BOOK CLUB

DIFFICULTY: ▪▫▫▫▫

You'd be forgiven for believing that book clubs are largely comprised of middle-aged, tweed-wearing, well-spoken ladies and gentlemen who meet once a week to discuss Thackeray over small cakes and sweet tea. There are, of course, plenty of book clubs out there  just like this, but there are so many more. A book club can take place anywhere – from trendy city bars to echoing town halls to student bedrooms to comfortable pubs to local parks – and a book club can gather together any type or style of person. The one constant is that books are involved. But these don't have to be the classics. They can be crime thrillers, Mills and Boon, travelogues, biographies or an eclectic mix of all the above and more. The wonderful thing about book clubs is that, generally, the members take it turn to select the books, so you'll be able to choose your own while also reading others which you might never have discovered otherwise. And, if you just can't find a book club in the local area which fits your tastes, why not start one yourself? It's a great way to widen your reading, but an even better way to regularly spend time meeting and talking (and, let's be frank here, drinking) with like-minded individuals.

SEE FAMILY

DIFFICULTY: ▪◻◻◻◻

If there's a member of your family who you feel you just don't see enough of, find some time to visit them. Perhaps there's a cousin in a different country who you've always promised to visit, or perhaps your brother and his family live just down the road but you only see them on important occasions. Make time for them. Whether you need to arrange an entire week to fly out and stay, or just half an hour to pop round for a cup of tea, spending time with family is important no matter how busy or successful you are. It's one of those things which many of us intend to do far more often than we actually *do*. And, if you're not sure who among your extended family you should make time for first, try an elder relative such as an aunt, uncle or grandparent. They'll appreciate it more than you might realise.

SEND A POSTCARD (OR FIVE)

DIFFICULTY: ▪◦◦◦◦

Buy five postcards and five stamps. Write and then send the five postcards to five friends. They can contain whatever you want (a joke, a story, a heartfelt message), and you can have lots of fun choosing images which will entertain and intrigue the recipients (there are some *very* bizarre postcards out there). Above all, send them to the five friends you would most like to receive a postcard back from.

NO-PHONE-TIME CHALLENGE

Lock your phone in a box and put the key somewhere difficult to reach. This creates an effective obstacle, and if you break through the obstacle you'll know you're also breaking your rule.

HAVE A BARBECUE

DIFFICULTY: ▪▪◻◻◻

A barbecue is always fun, but when you bring your friends together to make a special effort and share the work, the resulting party is even better. The first thing you'll need to do is gather your friends and explain the plan. The best barbecues are rarely solitary pursuits. They require help and camaraderie. Next, decide on your location. Your (or a friend's) garden is perfect, but if you want to get out to your nearest beach, check first that they allow open fires. Then, decide who will bring what, and allocate items to each member of the group. You will need (at the very least) the following:

> ▶ Firewood and/or charcoal
> ▶ Kindling and/or firelighters to get the fire going and some stones to contain it
> ▶ Utensils for cooking and eating (this can simply be a set of skewers)
> ▶ Food (very important, that one)
> ▶ Beverages (perhaps less important than food, but only marginally so)

Once you are all together, arrange the stones in a circle and build a small preliminary fire from the kindling (and perhaps some paper to get it going). Once this has taken, you can start to add the larger wood until it is roaring, and then (if you have it) the charcoal to maintain a steady heat. Then impale your food on skewers and roast each piece over the open flames. It will all require perhaps a whole evening's worth of effort to organise and implement, but it'll taste so good at the end.

MAKE NEW FRIENDS

DIFFICULTY: ■◻◻◻◻

As the range of activities across the UK builds, so too does the opportunity to find and make new friends. For this, it's forgivable to begin by using the internet to find websites which match people on a platonic rather than a romantic basis. But if you're a die-hard unplugger, you can still find new and like-minded friends the old-fashioned way – that is, by reading and responding to the pinned-up posts on boards in cafes, shops and hostels.

If you love your friends but find that your interests have diverged from theirs in recent years, or if you're new to an area and don't know anyone else who lives there, using websites or pin-board posts can be a wonderful way of meeting people who share the same interests as you. Societies and groups abound across the UK, so whether you're interested in cinema or horticulture, reading or running, biking or hiking, it's never been easier to hook up with others who like to spend their free time in exactly the same way as you do.

GO OUT ON THE TOWN

DIFFICULTY: ▪◻◻◻◻

This might seem like an obvious one – but when was the last time you properly went out with your mates? Even if you're lucky enough to see your friends on a regular basis, you might still find that it's increasingly easy to spend that time in one of your houses, perhaps with a movie and pizza, or a few bottles of wine or ale. Going out doesn't just require huge amounts of co-ordination and good timing, it probably also requires money, babysitters, and the length of time the following day that it now takes you to recover from a hangover. It's not that going out becomes less desirable as you get older, it's that it becomes more difficult to manage.

But that's no reason to stop altogether. Indeed, when you can fit all the pieces of the puzzle together in such a way that you and your friends *can* go out, then it makes the experience all the more worthwhile. Whatever your destination – be it a restaurant, a bar or even a nightclub – having a good night out with your closest friends is a wonderful and heartening antidote to the stresses of everyday life.

CHAPTER 5

EXPERIMENT WITH NEW HOBBIES

| PHONE | OFF ||| |
| CREATIVITY | ||| ON |

INTRODUCTION

Hobbies are remarkably important, perhaps more than we give them credit for. They can be as simple or as demanding as you want them to be, and you can undertake them at whatever level of expertise you choose. The beautiful thing about them is that they place no expectations on you (unlike most other areas of life), and whether they're meaningful or silly or intense or productive is entirely up to you. What they should never be, however, is boring – for this would defy the point of them entirely. So if you're finding that your usual hobbies just aren't enthralling you as much as they used to, have a look through these ideas. There are so many clubs and groups and societies and courses available these days that you really can learn and do whatever you want… all you need is the inclination!

DIG IN

DIFFICULTY: ▪▪▫▫▫

Whether you have an acre of land at your disposal, a tiny backyard or even just a windowsill, gardening is a peaceful and surprisingly empowering way to spend your free time. Growing and nurturing plant life is a beautiful way of reconnecting with nature, whether it involves the meticulous care of a eucalyptus tree or the seeding of your first tomato plant. Garden centres offer a vast array of flora in varying stages of life, and many also give away plants which are deemed to be at the end of their season – with the right care and love, these can be fostered back to life. For those who have little space, a window box of flowers makes an attractive display, and, even if you don't have a windowsill, indoor plants such as cacti and bonsai trees demand little care but can offer much aesthetic beauty amid  your furniture and gadgets. And, for those who live in cities, an allotment can often become both a rewarding pursuit and a wellspring of organically sourced food.

UNLEASH YOUR INNER DOODLER

DIFFICULTY: ▪◌◌◌

It can be easy to think that some of us can draw and some of us can't. Those who can't often push their own artistic sensibilities out of their lives and use a pen or pencil purely to write and a paintbrush purely to varnish the fence. But, whether you can draw or not, you have a little artist inside of you regardless. There are myriad ways of unleashing that inner artist, and one of the cheapest and simplest is by doodling. All you need is some paper and a pen or pencil and you can start. Cartoon characters are always fun (whether they're famous or your own), especially when rendered into short comic strips. Or you can simultaneously find your inner peace *and* create beautifully intricate drawings by following the Zentangle Method (you have permission to look this up online at www.zentangle.com).

SPLASH OUT WITH SOME PAINTS

DIFFICULTY: ▪◻◻◻◻

Doodling is plenty of fun, but if you want to get more colourful, more lively and just more *messy*, it might be time to invest in a palette of paints. You don't have to be the next Rembrandt or Renoir to paint – you can be as abstract as you like. In fact, sometimes it's far more rewarding that way. One deeply enjoyable form of abstract painting involves putting on a piece of music which stirs you emotionally (if you can't think of any, Ravel's *Boléro* is perfect) and then splashing your paints on to paper or canvas in whatever fashion you feel fits the music most appropriately.

TAKE YOUR BRUSH SKILLS TO THE NEXT LEVEL

DIFFICULTY: ▪▪◌◌◌

If you know deep down that you are already an accomplished artist who can draw and paint with a fair amount of skill, there's still always room to improve. In fact, people who tend to be skilled in subjects such as fine art or music or literature often find that their learning will regularly 'plateau' – that is, they will reach a certain level of skill and then find it difficult to push beyond that level. It can be easy to remain on that plateau, but for those who like to push themselves up to the next level and beyond, one of the most effective ways is to  take up classes. Life drawing and still-life classes are some of the most readily available kinds, but there are plenty of others out there, too – from one-on-one tutelage to Open University courses to studies in specific disciplines such as impressionism or surrealism.

GET YOUR HANDS GREASY

DIFFICULTY: ▪▪◻◻◻

Taking your car into your local garage for a regular service can cost anywhere between £100 and £500 each time. But doing it yourself costs only a fraction of that price. Online tutorials can provide a good starting point for servicing an engine, but there are also  a number of part-time college courses which offer hands-on lessons for those who want to learn how to do it themselves. Once you start to understand your way around an engine, you might want to extend that knowledge to the rest of your car. Again, there are many courses which can help you achieve this goal, and the more you learn the less you'll have to pay for your next MOT.

NO-PHONE-TIME CHALLENGE

Next time you go out, intentionally leave your phone at home (as long as it's safe to do so, of course!).

JOIN A BAND

DIFFICULTY: ▪▪▮▯▯

Have you ever stood in front of the mirror with a tennis racket and mimed the lead-guitar solo to a rock classic? Have you ever sung so loudly and with such passion in your car to the radio that other drivers passing you have begun to point and laugh? Have you ever air-drummed to a beat so frenetically that your arms ached for the rest of the day? Then maybe it's time to join a band.

There are a plethora of available opportunities for the aspiring musician, no matter what his or her level of talent might be. If you can sing but don't want to be the frontman, perhaps try and find a backing-singer role.

EXPERIMENT WITH NEW HOBBIES

If you can play an instrument but would rather a join a more low-key outfit, there are plenty of acoustic ensembles which play a range of styles on a variety of instruments. If you want to get out there and start gigging and even earning a little bit of spare money, you can join an established band or even form your own with a group of like-minded musicians. Either way, whether you want to delicately harmonise in a small room with others of the same ilk or want to smash out your latest riff in front of a packed pub, finding a band is the perfect way to actualise your musical ambitions.

SING

DIFFICULTY: ▪◻◻◻◻

A wonderful alternative to a band is the vocal choir. Choirs can be both a great way to learn to sing and a great way to continue practising your singing. Having others around you performing the same melody helps keep your pitch on track and gives you the confidence to sing loud and proud, which you might lack when on your own. There are a multitude of different types of choir – from classical to gospel to jazz to rock-and-pop. Just name the kind of music you'd like to sing, and no doubt you'll be able to find something suitable.

LEARN AN INSTRUMENT

DIFFICULTY: ▪▪▮▯▯

For those of you who can't play an instrument and can't sing (or have a sheer aversion to it) but still fancy being musical, there's a simple solution. Learn a new instrument. All right, maybe it's not that simple if you want to learn the harp or the cor anglais, but you can still become a musician without breaking the bank. Drumming circles and samba bands are fantastic for learning how to drum quickly and in a fun and sociable  setting. Popular string instruments such as guitars and ukuleles may look tough when you watch professionals make them cry and sing, but you'll be amazed at the hundreds of well-known songs you can play with just three chords. Perhaps you even spent some time during childhood learning an instrument, only to put it aside and forget about it as you grew up. If so, now's the time to pick it up again – regular practice is sometimes all it takes for those old muscle-memories to kick back in.

ATTEND AN OPEN-MIC NIGHT

DIFFICULTY: ∎∎◻◻◻

Many pubs, clubs, cafes and bars hold regular open-mic nights for new and aspiring performers. Whether you're a budding musician, poet or stand-up comedian, these are the perfect opportunity to try out your skills in front of a live audience. Most open-mic nights are free to attend and offer a 5–20-minute slot for anyone who wants to have a go. And, because the performers are generally non-professionals, audiences at open-mic nights tend to be supportive and welcoming, so that even the most timid of performers can be nurtured as they blossom within their chosen artform.

PULL THE OTHER ONE

Bell-ringing (or campanology) is an ancient art which has provided the soundtrack to many landscapes across the world for the last 1,500 years. Getting into bell-ringing is easier than you might think. There are numerous bell-ringing clubs and societies out there. Most are free to join and, once you express an interest, you will quite literally be shown the ropes. Beginners are taught the various techniques of the art before joining a bell-ringing team, at which point they are then guided through the intricacies of change-ringing (following a pattern of ringing with others to create a chiming melody). It's a wonderful exercise for those interested in music – from professionals to novices – as well as being wonderful *exercise* in itself.

GET ON THE AIRWAVES

DIFFICULTY: ▪▪▫▫▫

If you've ever been interested in getting into media, there are a whole host of community radio stations that are looking for local people to get involved. These tend to run on charitable donations and the odd bit of advertising. You won't be paid for working for a community radio station, but the experience you can garner from one is considerable. Maybe you want to be in the limelight as a DJ or stand back a little but still be heard as a news, weather or traffic reporter. Perhaps you'd like to learn the ins and outs of radio production and sound engineering, or just like to be behind the scenes but still a part of the magic in a research or assistant capacity. Whatever your preference, community radio stations are a great way of pursuing a hobby or gaining experience for a future career in the medium.

CHAPTER 6

EXPAND YOUR MIND

BOREDOM	
FASCINATION	

INTRODUCTION

Have you ever heard that old saying – that the brain is a muscle and needs to be exercised? This isn't strictly true, because the brain is an organ rather than a muscle, but the sentiment of the saying is still pertinent. Your brain needs its own form of exercise to ensure that it remains stimulated and, like all the other organs in your body, healthy. There are myriad ways you can challenge your brain – from a five-minute game of Countdown to a full university degree. For more information on both of these, and for plenty of suggestions in between, read on.

MEDITATE

DIFFICULTY: ▪▪◻◻◻

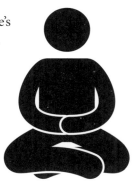

Meditation is the act of clearing one's mind and floating the consciousness upon nothingness. It may seem daunting at first, but with only a small amount of practice you can start to feel the benefits of meditation. It is, after all, a skill, and like any other skill the more you do it the better you become at it. And, once you can achieve a stable meditative state, ten minutes of it can be as relaxing and as rejuvenating as a two-hour nap.

Start small. Find a quiet place where you won't be disturbed, draw the curtains, turn off the lights and anything which might emit sound (such as your phone), and then either lie on your back or sit up straight. Close your eyes, ensure your breathing is deep and full, and then try to clear your mind and think of nothing at all. Don't worry if this only lasts a few seconds. Keep practising and you *will* get better at it. Before long, you'll be able to enjoy the many benefits which meditation can bring to life, such as lower stress levels, a heightening of the ability to think calmly and rationally, a surge in willpower, and much more.

ENTER A WORLD OF PUZZLES

DIFFICULTY: ▪▪◻◻◻

For many people, the first (and sometimes only) kind of puzzle they can think of is the crossword – or, if they're feeling a little exotic, a sudoku. But these are just two of a vast array of puzzle types which exist for you to solve. The beautiful thing about puzzles is that they are far more satisfying to complete with a simple pen and paper than on a computer or other device. The very act of scribbling, crossing out and making notes or workings in the margins only adds to the sense of achievement one feels on completion. There are a vast array of books and magazines packed with word searches, sangaku, spot the difference, anagrams, sokoban – and, of course, the inimitable crossword and sudoku – so it's as easy to find them as it is to dive straight in and get puzzling.

CHALLENGE YOUR FRIENDS

DIFFICULTY: ▪▪◻◻◻

1. Pick a group of friends who love puzzles and teasers.

2. Each friend has to create their own mentally stimulating challenge for the rest of the group. These could be brainteasers, pub quizzes, find-the-country challenges on blank maps, anagrams, ciphers, codes or anything else you can think of.

3. Distribute your challenges among the group. Each person has to try and complete every challenge in the group except their own.

4. Share your results with each other. You could have two winners – the person who correctly completed the most challenges, and the person whose challenge was deemed the most difficult (and if this ends up being the same person, you should perhaps give them a prize, or maybe just 'forget' to invite them to the next round of challenges).

GET THREE-DIMENSIONAL

DIFFICULTY: ▪■◻◻◻

If you're more of a hands-on type of person, you might find that puzzles such as those listed in the previous two sections leave you bored rather than stimulated. If that's the case, don't worry – there are still plenty of physical puzzles which are ideal for the hands-on puzzler. Why not try a jigsaw, peg solitaire or a Rubik's Cube? Or you could even seek out those mini-puzzles which always seem to turn up at Christmas (the ones where balls go in holes, or blocks of wood go in stacks, or lengths of string go in loops). They may well be utterly frustrating, but these games can also be insidiously addictive and keep you entertained for hours.

JUGGLE

DIFFICULTY: ▪▪▪◻◻

When juggling, it's difficult to think of anything at all as your brain co-ordinates with your body in the single act of moving three balls from hand to hand. It's meditative, and many people claim that a quick juggle is a great way of refocusing and recharging the mind. If you can't juggle, don't worry. It may seem hard at first, but it can be learned, and even the act of learning it can be an engaging and powerful cognitive stimulant.

1. Start with one ball (if you don't have any juggling balls, tennis balls will do – and if you don't have those, apples or oranges are a perfect weight and size). Practise throwing it from one hand to another. Try to ensure that the peak of the ball's arc is at your eye-line.

2. Introduce the second ball. Throw the first ball from your dominant hand and, once it reaches your eye-line, throw the second ball from your other hand. Catch both and repeat the exercise until you are comfortable with it.

3. Introduce the third ball in exactly the same way. Keep doing it until you get to the point where you can throw and catch all three balls.

4. Once you can do that, you'll find the rhythm in the throws and catches, and all you need to do is maintain that rhythm.

TRY OUT AN EVENING CLASS

DIFFICULTY: ▪▪◻◻◻

In the arena of adult education, degrees are not the be-all and end-all. In fact, a massive variety of educational opportunities exists for adults who just miss the very act of learning and want to learn more. Evening classes and short courses can help you let out your creative side while also having fun – especially if you take one with a friend.

Maybe you've always had a secret interest in a particular area of the arts or engineering or science and wouldn't mind deepening your knowledge of it. Or maybe you just fancy having a go at something slightly wacky or out of your comfort zone. You may not even be aware of how many different courses are out there, ready and waiting. On the opposite page are just a few from the colleges in my local area. All it takes is the will to look. And who knows, that one quick look might lead to a fun hobby, an enduring passion, or even a brand new career. Secret agent, anyone?

garment making

glass blowing

aqua rehabilitation

yoga for the not very flexible

tap dancing

the joy of singing (intermediate)

medicines from the hedgerow

learn to be assertive

create a living willow fence

secret agent studies

PLAY SPONTANEOUS NUMBER GAMES

DIFFICULTY: ▪▪◻◻◻

One way of keeping your brain spry and sprightly is by playing arithmetic games in your head using random numbers in your immediate vicinity. Here are some ideas:

▶ Roughly work out the total number of words in the book you're currently reading by counting the number of words and the number of lines on one page and multiplying them. Then multiply this by the number of pages.

▶ Fill up your car with fuel. Note how many litres you use. Convert this to gallons in your head (one gallon is roughly four and a half litres). Make a note of how many miles you can drive on that single tank. Using the two figures, work out how many miles-to-the-gallon your car does.

▶ If you don't drive, whenever you are a passenger in a car or bus, try to keep a simultaneous tally of all the black, white and silver cars that you pass. To make it even harder, add in different colours and see if you can keep up.

▶ Find the Prime Number Objects in your kitchen. How many forks, saucepans, teabags or wooden spoons are there in your kitchen? Are any of them a prime number?

NO-PHONE-TIME CHALLENGE

In your free time, don't leave your phone out on the sofa or on the table beside you, but intentionally put it somewhere out of sight, perhaps even in another room. This will help it to fade from your mind.

STARGAZE

DIFFICULTY: ■■◻◻◻

Gazing up at the stars is a pastime as old as human history. Around 3000 BCE, the Mesopotamians began to inscribe on stone and clay tablets the constellations they could see. Who knows what they must have thought when they stared up into space on a cloudless night and contemplated the heavens? Today, there are 88 recognised constellations, comprising 42 animals, 17 human or mythological characters and 29 inanimate objects. Learning where and when the constellations can be found, what they are named after and which stars populate them can become an interesting and even obsessive pursuit. A telescope will allow you to see deep into the starry sky, but even if you don't have a telescope, simply reading a good encyclopaedia will give you a decent introduction to the constellations. If you're a beginner, here's the Top 5 constellations to look out for and learn about:

1. Orion (the Hunter)
2. Taurus (the Bull)
3. Gemini (the Twins)
4. Ursa Minor (the Little Bear)
5. Ursa Major (the Big Bear)

As well as looking for these constant features of our skies, keep a lookout for passing meteor showers which will enliven your nightscape with a celestial lightshow, or find out when the International Space Station will next be passing overhead and marvel that there are human beings inside it. And, if you're in it for the long haul, stick around until 2061, when Halley's Comet will next fire across our skies.

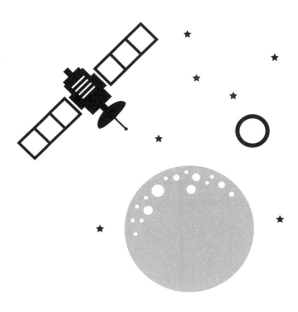

GET THAT DEGREE

DIFFICULTY: ▪▪❚❚▯

For many people, one of their most abiding regrets is that they never quite got the qualifications they had imagined when they were young. If this is one of your regrets, bear in mind that it doesn't have to be.

Today, both part-time and full-time courses are readily available for anyone who wants to take them on. Universities are seeing a huge surge in mature students and, for those who can't commit to a full-time programme, the Open University offers degrees which can be undertaken at a much more leisurely rate. Equally, if there isn't a university in your local area, distance-learning courses are available whereby tutors can send you packs of resources to be completed, returned and then marked. And, if it's a particular GCSE or A-Level you're after, your local college will doubtless have information and perhaps even the exact course you're after.

START A JOURNAL

DIFFICULTY: ▪◌◌◌◌

The famous saying is, 'Everyone has a novel inside of them.' But I prefer this version, from author Neil Gaiman: 'Everyone has a secret world inside of them.'

Tackling a whole novel can be an incredibly daunting prospect (even for full-time novelists), but exploring that secret world inside you doesn't have to involve such an enormous undertaking.

For many first-time writers, one of the most immediate and accessible forms of writing is journaling. Keeping a journal or diary is a magnificent way of discovering your own voice and being able to see the ups and downs of life from a slightly more detached viewpoint. It can be cathartic and it can be liberating, and it can certainly help you channel your secret world through the written word.

WRITE A POEM

DIFFICULTY: ▪▪◻◻◻

Poetry really can be anything you like. It doesn't have to rhyme. It doesn't even have to be *written down* – it's exceptionally versatile and can be and mean largely whatever you want. Nevertheless, if you fancy a bit of a challenge, there are some poetic forms which you might want to have a go at, ranging from the simple to the absurdly difficult. Each has its own set of rules (which are sometimes flexible and sometimes absolutely mandatory). Below are some suggestions – all you have to do is choose one, have a (quick) online search for the particular rules, then whip out your pen and paper and get writing.

- ▶ Limerick
- ▶ Acrostic
- ▶ Haiku
- ▶ Sonnet
- ▶ Landay
- ▶ Pantoum

WRITE WITH OTHERS

DIFFICULTY: ▪◦◦◦◦

We often think of writing as a solitary pursuit but, in fact, writing can be a fun way of getting together with friends and even making new friends. Writing groups have become almost as ubiquitous as book clubs in local communities, and they are always on the lookout for new members, from novices to professionals. Similarly, there are national writing challenges such as NaNoWriMo (the National Novel Writing Month) every November where you can derive encouragement for your writing by meeting and sharing with other writers from all across the world. If you just want to meet up with a friend, set aside an hour of writing time, brew a pot of tea, crack open some biscuits and then *just write* – even that can be a fulfilling way of expressing yourself creatively whilst revelling in good company.

CHAPTER 7

EXPRESS YOUR COMPASSION

SELFISHNESS	OFF |||
KINDNESS	||| ON

INTRODUCTION

One of the most satisfying and fulfilling ways of making the most of your free time can be by helping others. In short, by being kind. This doesn't necessarily mean that you need to head straight down to your local charity shop and volunteer for the next 12-hour shift (although I'm sure they'd be grateful if you did!). Simply holding open the door for a stranger, buying flowers for a loved one or getting involved in a community project can make all the difference.

DONATE TO A FOOD BANK

DIFFICULTY: ▪◻◻◻◻

The use of, and the need for, food banks in the UK has risen dramatically over the past few years. The Trussell Trust – the country's largest food bank organisation – has gone from running 56 food banks in 2009 to a staggering 445 in 2014.

While there may not be a food bank itself which you can volunteer for in your local area, it's easy enough to donate to one of the food bank organisations. Most mainstream supermarkets have baskets or boxes near the checkouts where people's donations of food can be collected and then transported to the nearest food bank, where it is then given to those in need. This has helped make the act of donating extremely easy and also extremely rewarding (many people believe that charity should begin at home, and food banks are following that maxim immaculately). Donations can be as simple and affordable as a tin of beans or a pack of pasta, or they can be as extravagant and exotic as a selection of rare pickles and spices. A can of chopped tomatoes will do. So will a grow-your-own-vegetables seed pack. And, when added to your regular weekly shop, you'll barely notice the difference.

VOLUNTEER

DIFFICULTY: ▪▫▫▫▫

Do you ever wish that you could give more to charity? Do you watch the adverts and see the posters and read the mail sent to you, yet despair because you just can't afford to give? Well, charities don't just need money, they need time, too – and if your funds can't stretch to financial donations, maybe your time can stretch to a different kind of donation. From working the till at a shop to campaigning and leafletting, to helping stock a warehouse, to going abroad and engaging with the cause first-hand, there are a multitude of ways in which you can volunteer for charity work. And it's not a purely altruistic pursuit. There are so many charities doing wonderful and invaluable things in the world today, and by choosing a cause which you genuinely believe in and support, you will make your volunteering experience all the more worthwhile and beneficial for yourself, contributing to your own wellbeing whilst helping others at the same time.

GIVE 1 PER CENT

DIFFICULTY: ▪◻◻◻◻

How much is just 1 per cent of your monthly earnings? Is it a figure which you can imagine perhaps living without? If so, then why not donate it? For many of us, that 1 per cent is entirely negligible, but for those on the receiving end, our 1 per cent can mean the world. And imagine if we all gave just 1 per cent of our earnings to those who truly needed it. The world would be, without doubt, a better place. If you've always wanted to give to charity but have never known how much you should give, 1 per cent is a great place to start. Whether you dedicate it to a single cause or spread it across a multitude, that 1 per cent will change lives without making a noticeable dent in your bank balance.

GET INVOLVED WITH YOUR LOCAL SCHOOL

DIFFICULTY: ▪◻◻◻◻

Schools are funded by budgets allocated to them by local authorities based largely on the number of children who attend. Nevertheless, it is common for schools to reach out to their local communities for financial help – whether it's to assist with staffing, educational trips or providing resources. If you have children who attend your local school or you're friends with teachers who work there, it makes sense to get involved and help out. But even if you're just interested in supporting your local community, there are few more rewarding ways to do so than by helping your local school.

If you have solid organisational skills, you could offer to organise a fundraising event such as a fete, coffee morning, raffle or fun run. Or, if you love working with children, you could offer some of your time as a teaching assistant. There are many levels to this job and most require some form of training, but if you don't have any and still want to help out, you could spend an hour each Thursday morning reading with Key Stage 1 children or an hour each Tuesday afternoon helping out with the football team. Whatever you wish to offer, it is highly likely that your local school will be immensely grateful for it.

FUNDRAISE

DIFFICULTY: ▪▪◻◻◻

There are so many ways in which you can fundraise for your favourite charity, and only a few of them involve using the internet (such as the notorious ice-bucket challenge). Beyond the technological landscape, the age-old beauties of a sponsored walk or run are still classics, but fundraising can be as adventurous, as spirited or as silly as you want it to be. You can do a sponsored silence or keep a swear jar. You can climb a mountain (or three) for charity. You can create an event such as a concert or gig with a local band or choir. You can set up a stall in town and give people information about your cause in return for donations. You can enlist your workmates in a charity auction. You can hold a car-boot sale or yard sale to sell off your unwanted possessions and give the takings away. You can even shave off all your hair or wear a ridiculous outfit on a night out.

HELP OUT AT AN ANIMAL SHELTER

DIFFICULTY: ▪▫▫▫▫

Animal shelters are largely staffed by trained professionals, but they welcome volunteers who can walk a dog for an hour a week or spend an afternoon giving their cats some much-needed attention. If you love animals but don't have the time or commitment for a pet, this can be a rewarding way of spending your free time. And who knows, you might just fall in love with that mongrel or moggy you've come to know and realise that there is enough time in your life for them, after all.

PERFORM RANDOM ACTS OF KINDNESS

DIFFICULTY: ∎◻◻◻◻

A random act of kindness can be your own good deed for the day. Indulging your kind side randomly and regularly will not only brighten someone else's day, it'll also brighten your own. Here are a few suggestions:

- Hold the door open for someone entering or exiting wherever you are.
- Have a chat with the rough sleeper you often see in your locale.
- Help someone carry their shopping bags home.
- Offer to guide an elderly person across a busy road.
- Put a pound in a collection box.
- Allow other drivers past at a busy junction.
- Take some old stationery or some of your kids' old toys down to a nearby residential home for children.
- Donate all those old clothes you never wear and books you never read to your local charity shop.
- Go out and pick up litter, and then recycle as much as you can.

NO-PHONE-TIME CHALLENGE

Have a 'No phones after...' rule at home and then – crucially – stick to it. And be sure to properly turn your phones off: don't just put them on silent or flight mode.

CHAPTER 8

ENJOY BEING SILLY

SERIOUSNESS

PLAYFULNESS

INTRODUCTION

If anyone ever tells you that being silly is just for children, immediately moonwalk away from them whilst singing 'Bohemian Rhapsody'. Imbecility, immaturity, puerility – call it what you like, but the fact is that, as an adult, you have every right to be silly. In fact, you've earned it. And it's bloody good fun, too.

CATCH PEANUTS

DIFFICULTY: ▪▪◻◻◻

Learn to catch peanuts in your mouth. You may need a very big bag of peanuts before you master this ancient and awe-inspiring skill.

TRANSFORM YOURSELF

DIFFICULTY: ▪▫▫▫▫

Go into a vintage or second-hand clothes shop and try on clothes that a different version of you might wear. Could you have been a 1970s disco king or queen? Or a genteel village detective? Or a hip-hop artist with more jewellery than sense? Find the right clothes, and decide for yourself. This is a great way of finding something sensational for an upcoming fancy dress party, vintage fair or theme night.

GARGLE

DIFFICULTY: ∎◻◻◻◻

1. Dress in clothes you don't mind getting wet.
2. Fill a half-pint glass with tap water.
3. Empty a quarter of it into your mouth.
4. Don't swallow.
5. Angle your head back and make sure the water doesn't pass your tonsils.
6. Gargle the theme tune to your favourite television programme.

If you laugh or if a single droplet of water dribbles on to your chin, spit the water out and go back to Step 1.

(This also makes a fun – and, of course, silly – game. Try it with friends and see if you can all guess each other's tunes.)

BEARD UP

DIFFICULTY: ∎◦◌◌◌

Buy a face-painting kit. Experiment with a number of different beards. Here are some you might want to choose from:

- ▶ Goatee
- ▶ Chinstrap
- ▶ Mutton chops
- ▶ Handlebar moustache
- ▶ Soul patch
- ▶ Fu Manchu
- ▶ Horseshoe moustache
- ▶ Neck beard
- ▶ Pencil moustache
- ▶ Full hipster beard

When you've found the one which suits you the least, wear it for the next six hours.

INVENT STORIES

DIFFICULTY: ▪◻◻◻◻

Whenever you find yourself among a group of people – waiting at the train station, in a pub, on a bus – look at those around you and invent secret, exciting lives for them (but try not to stare too much!). This is a perfect game for anyone who's interested in writing – the personalities you create could go on to feature in your upcoming stories.

SET A NEW TREND

DIFFICULTY: ▪▪▮▮▮

See how long you can go wearing a shower cap. If you can make it all day, you're a better person than I am.

IMPRESS

DIFFICULTY: ▪▪◻◻◻

Performing and guessing impressions can make for a great game with friends, but you can also do them by yourself if you just fancy brightening up a quiet day. Here are some impressions you can try:

- ▶ Sean Connery doing an impression of Roger Moore
- ▶ A newsreader reporting on a royal wedding whilst trying to hold back a fit of giggles
- ▶ A young dolphin who wants to be a tap dancer when he grows up
- ▶ The mother of teenage triplets who has just won the lottery
- ▶ Each of the teenage triplets
- ▶ A cow who hates the taste of grass
- ▶ A Premier League footballer who scores a goal whilst desperate for the toilet
- ▶ A chef who's just found out that Gordon Ramsay is eating in his restaurant
- ▶ A dog who won't give its stick back to its owner

HAVE A BANANA

DIFFICULTY: ▪◻◻◻◻

Literally.

CHECKLIST

CHAPTER 1: EXPLORE YOUR WORLD

- ☐ Turn right
- ☐ Visit the local park
- ☐ Reconnect with the past
- ☐ Forage
- ☐ Go camping
- ☐ Explore your national heritage
- ☐ Beachcomb

CHAPTER 2: EXERCISE YOUR BODY

- ☐ Walk
- ☐ Run
- ☐ Cycle for pleasure
- ☐ Cycle for fitness
- ☐ Try silly cycling
- ☐ Learn a martial art
- ☐ Join a local sports team
- ☐ Surf
- ☐ Relive old childhood games

CHECKLIST

CHAPTER 3: EMBARK ON NEW ADVENTURES

- ☐ Take on the zombies
- ☐ Wing-walk
- ☐ Go wine-tasting
- ☐ Go coasteering
- ☐ Go paintballing
- ☐ Go tubing
- ☐ Get wild with theatre
- ☐ Go zorbing

CHAPTER 4: EMBRACE YOUR SOCIAL LIFE

- ☐ Arrange to see an old friend
- ☐ Play dinner carousel
- ☐ Join a book club
- ☐ See family
- ☐ Send a postcard (or five)
- ☐ Have a barbecue
- ☐ Make new friends
- ☐ Go out on the town

CHAPTER 5: EXPERIMENT WITH NEW HOBBIES

- ☐ Dig in
- ☐ Unleash your inner doodler
- ☐ Splash out with some paints
- ☐ Take your brush skills to the next level
- ☐ Get your hands greasy
- ☐ Join a band

- ☐ Sing
- ☐ Learn an instrument
- ☐ Attend an open-mic night
- ☐ Pull the other one
- ☐ Get on the airwaves

CHAPTER 6: EXPAND YOUR MIND

- ☐ Meditate
- ☐ Enter a world of puzzles
- ☐ Challenge your friends
- ☐ Get three-dimensional
- ☐ Juggle
- ☐ Try out an evening class
- ☐ Play spontaneous number games
- ☐ Stargaze
- ☐ Get that degree
- ☐ Start a journal
- ☐ Write a poem
- ☐ Write with others

CHAPTER 7: EXPRESS YOUR COMPASSION

- ☐ Donate to a food bank
- ☐ Volunteer
- ☐ Give 1 per cent
- ☐ Get involved with your local school
- ☐ Fundraise
- ☐ Help out at an animal shelter
- ☐ Perform random acts of kindness

CHAPTER 8: ENJOY BEING SILLY

- ☐ Catch peanuts
- ☐ Transform yourself
- ☐ Gargle
- ☐ Beard up
- ☐ Invent stories
- ☐ Set a new trend
- ☐ Impress
- ☐ Have a banana

NOTES

HOW TO
UNPLUG
YOUR CHILD

101 WAYS TO HELP YOUR KIDS TURN OFF
THEIR GADGETS AND ENJOY REAL LIFE

LIAT HUGHES JOSHI

GET YOUR SHIT TOGETHER

HOW TO CHANGE YOUR LIFE BY TIDYING UP YOUR STUFF & SORTING OUT YOUR HEAD SPACE

Vicki Vrint

ISBN: 978 1 84953 794 0   Hardback   £6.99

ORGANISE YOUR STUFF AND ORGANISE YOUR LIFE – YOU'LL SOON SEE THE RESULTS.

This book tells you *exactly* how to get your sh*t together, so you can be the best version of yourself.

Use its winning blend of super-achievable life hacks, motivating quotations and lots of good sh*t to kick-start your transformation.

Have you enjoyed this book?

If so, why not write a review on your favourite website?
If you're interested in finding out more about
our books, find us on Facebook at
SUMMERSDALE PUBLISHERS
and follow us on Twitter at
@SUMMERSDALE.

Thanks very much for buying this Summersdale book.

WWW.SUMMERSDALE.COM